The publishers are grateful for permission to reproduce the following material:

"I Talk with the Moon" originally appeared in *Instructor*, May 1985. Reprinted by permission of the author, who controls all rights.

"Morning Song" by Bobbi Katz; from *Poems for Small Friends* by Bobbi Katz, Random House, Inc.; copyright © Random House, Inc. 1989; reproduced by permission of the author.

"Wake Up" Zaro Weil 1989; from *Mud, Moon and Me*, Orchard Books, a division of The Watts Group; reproduced by kind permission of Orchard Books, 96 Leonard Street, London EC2A 4RH.

Illustrations from *A Cup of Starshine* by Jill Bennett, illustrations copyright © 1991 by Graham Percy, reproduced by permission of Harcourt Brace & Company.

Reprinted with the permission of Macmillan Publishing Company from *The Mousehole Cat* by Antonia Barber, illustrated by Nicola Bayley. Text copyright © 1990 Antonia Barber. Illustrations copyright © 1990 Nicola Bayley.

The Stopwatch by David Lloyd: copyright © 1986 by David Lloyd. Illustration copyright © 1986 by Penny Dale. Selection reprinted by permission of HarperCollins Publishers.

On Your Potty: copyright © 1991 by Virginia Miller. By permission of Greenwillow Books, a division of William Morrow & Company, Inc.

From *The Great Waldo Search* by Martin Handford. Copyright © 1989 by Martin Handford. By permission of Little, Brown and Company.

Reprinted with the permission of Aladdin Books, an imprint of Macmillan Publishing Company from *Tom and Pippo and the Washing Machine* written and illustrated by Helen Oxenbury. Text and illustrations copyright © 1988 Helen Oxenbury.

"Quack" said the Billygoat by Charles Causley: copyright © 1986 by Charles Causley. Illustration copyright © 1986 by Barbara Firth. Selection reprinted by permission of HarperCollins Publishers.

A Piece of Cake by Jill Murphy, copyright © 1989 by Jill Murphy. Reprinted by permission G. P. Putnam's Sons.

Sir Gawain and the Green Knight by Selina Hastings, illustrated by Juan Wijngaard. Text copyright © 1981 by Selina Hastings. Illustration copyright © 1981 by Juan Wijngaard. By permission of Lothrop, Lee & Shepard Books, a division of William Morrow & Company Inc.

From *Ragged Robin* by James Reeves; illustrated by Emma Chichester-Clark. Text copyright © 1961 by James Reeves; illustrations copyright © 1990 by Emma Chichester-Clark. By permission of Little, Brown and Company.

The Owl and the Pussycat, written by Edward Lear. Illustration copyright © 1991 by Louise Voce. By permission of Lothrop, Lee & Shepard Books, a division of William Morrow & Company, Inc.

From *First Things First* by Charlotte Voake. Copyright © 1988 by Charlotte Voake. By permission of Little, Brown and Company.

"The Tiger" by William Blake is reprinted with the permission of Macmillan Publishing Company from *Birds, Beasts and Fishes* selected by Anne Carter, illustrated by Reg Cartwright. Illustrations copyright © 1991 Reg Cartwright.

Reprinted with the permission of Macmillan Publishing Company from *In the Middle of the Night* by Kathy Henderson, illustrated by Jennifer Eachus. Text copyright © 1992 Kathy Henderson. Illustrations copyright © 1992 Jennifer Eachus.

First U.S. edition 1994   Published in Great Britain in 1994 by Walker Books Ltd., London.

Library of Congress Cataloging-in-Publication Data   (Revised for vol.3)

Big Bear's treasury.

Originally published: London: Walker Books, 1990. An illustrated collection of stories and poems by such authors and illustrators as Colin McNaughton, Helen Oxenbury, Martin Handford and Charlotte Voake.
1. Children's literature. 2. Literature—Collections.
PZ5. B4349 1992   808.8199282   91-71859
ISBN 1-56402-002-9 (v. 1)

ISBN 1-56402-113-0 (v. 2)   ISBN 1-56402-309-5 (v. 3)

10 9 8 7 6 5 4 3 2 1

Printed in Italy

CANDLEWICK PRESS, 2067 MASSACHUSETTS AVENUE, CAMBRIDGE, MASSACHUSETTS 02140

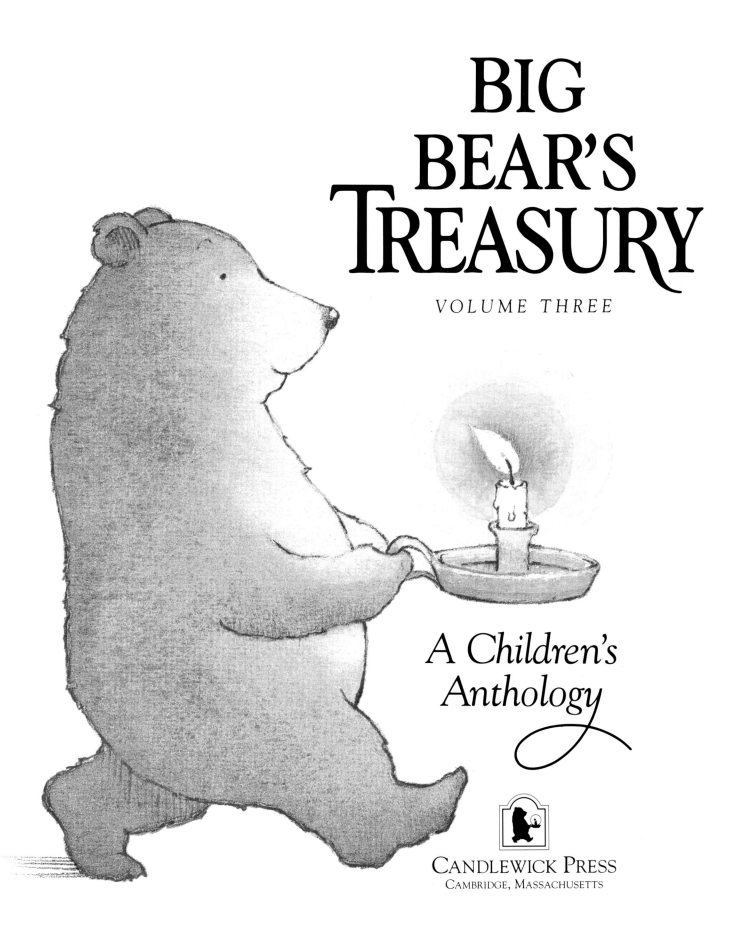

BIG
BEAR'S
TREASURY

VOLUME THREE

A Children's
Anthology

CANDLEWICK PRESS
CAMBRIDGE, MASSACHUSETTS

CONTENTS

This book of stories, poems, and pictures is the third treasury to light up with the glow from Big Bear's candle. Thirty-two favorite books, by the world's finest writers and artists for children, are here in one volume. Sometimes they're here from beginning to end, sometimes a little bit has been picked out; always they offer a new, quite distinct way of saying and seeing things. Turning from page to page, you never know what may be coming next.

Many of the books gathered to make this collection already exist on their own, inside their own covers. If you find selections you particularly like, you can look for more books by the writers and illustrators in bookstores and libraries. Discovering authors and artists you love will help you find more and more books to enjoy.

But this book is special. It glows with a light all its own. Turn the pages and bask in the glow. Then Big Bear can be sure that you're having a truly wonderful time.

Poems from

A CUP OF
STARSHINE

edited by Jill Bennett
illustrated by Graham Percy

I TALK WITH THE MOON

I talk with the moon, said the owl
    While she lingers over my tree
I talk with the moon, said the owl
    And the night belongs to me.

I talk with the sun, said the wren
    As soon as he starts to shine
I talk with the sun, said the wren
    And the day is mine.

Beverly McLoughland

WAKE UP

Wake up
Morning
Has
Galloped
Bareback
All night to
Get here

Zaro Weil

8

MORNING SONG

Today is a day to catch tadpoles.
Today is a day to explore.
Today is a day to get started.
Come on! Let's not sleep anymore.

Outside the sunbeams are dancing.
The leaves sing a rustling song.
Today is a day for adventures,
And I hope that you'll come along!

Bobbi Katz

9

Ben and the Bear

by Chris Riddell

One day Ben was bored. He put on a big winter coat. He put on a floppy hat. Then he set off into the snow. After a while he met a bear. The bear said, "What a lovely coat." Ben said, "Come home for a tea party."
Some of the way the bear carried Ben.

Some of the way Ben tried to carry the bear. The bear took Ben's coat. Ben and the bear sat down at the table. The bear poured the tea.

Ben passed the sugar cubes. The bear ate them all up. They ate some bread.

And then they ate some
honey. The bear said,
"Let's dance." So they
did. Ben said,
"What a
mess!" The
bear said,
"Let's play
clean up." They washed
up. They put the dishes
away. They folded the
tablecloth. Ben said,
"That looks neat." The
bear said, "What about
the coat?" Ben said, "You
can have the coat."
The bear said,
"Tomorrow you must
come to tea at
my house."

The Amazing Story of
NOAH'S ARK
by Marcia Williams

Many, many summers and winters ago, God became angry with the world because people had become so cruel. They were stealing and lying, cheating and fighting, so God decided to send a fearful flood to drown them all. Everyone except Noah and his family. For Noah was a good, kind man.

"Noah," said God, "I will save all your family and a male and female of every animal.

Build a great ark of cypress wood, three stories high. Then fill it with food."

Noah and his family worked hard building the ark. They chopped down trees and sawed the logs.

They hammered and sanded, then covered the wood with tar to stop the ark from leaking.

People laughed at Noah. They thought he was crazy talking of floods and building an ark.

But Noah worked on until the ark was ready. Then God told him to start loading it up.

Noah thought he might have trouble catching all the animals. But he didn't, for God had told them to go to Noah and climb aboard his ark.

The animals went in two by two—giraffes and birds and elephants, rhinos and camels and ladybugs, bears and sheep and spotted lizards, leopards and rabbits and lions and seals, zebras and snakes, a cow and a bull and a pair of goats, walruses, guinea hens, and pigs, and all the tiny insects, which Noah could hardly see.

It was hard work squeezing them all in!

But when the first drops of rain fell, the last insect found a bed

and the great doors were slammed shut.

For forty days and forty nights the rain fell. The ark was lifted above the earth. The waters rose higher and higher until even the tallest mountain was covered. Not a creature on earth was still alive. And still it rained on and on.

For many days the ark drifted.

Then God sent a wind over the earth, and down, down, down, the waters went.

Finally, after seven long months, the ark came to rest on the top of Mount Ararat.

Noah opened a window and let out a raven. But it could find nowhere to land.

He opened the window again and sent out a dove. It flew far and wide but found nowhere to rest.

GOOD LUCK.

Seven days later Noah sent out the dove once more. All day he waited, hoping it would bring good news.

In the evening it returned to the ark. In its beak it carried an olive branch. This told Noah that soon the waters would dry. He waited another seven days and then sent out the dove again.

HOORAY!

This time it did not return to the ark. Noah opened the window and saw that the earth was dry. Everyone in the ark gave a mighty cheer, for they were saved.

Noah pushed open the great door. Out rushed his family and all the animals, joyful to walk on land again. Noah built an altar to thank God. God was so pleased that He promised Noah never to flood the world again.

A rainbow appeared as a sign of His promise. Noah was very happy to see this. He made a new home and planted a vineyard and lived to be a very great age with his family and all the creatures of the ark and their many children. So now, whenever it rains and you see a rainbow, you can remember the story of Noah.

WHO'S  BEEN SLEEPING

I ONCE SAW A FISH UP A TREE

I once saw a fish up a tree,
   And this fish he had legs, believe me.
     Said the monster, "I'll swear,
     I'm just taking the air."
Then he jumped down and ran off to sea.

MOM IS HAVING A BABY!

Mom is having a baby!
I'm shocked! I just can't see
What she wants another one for:
WHAT'S THE MATTER WITH ME!?

WHO'S BEEN SLEEPING IN MY PORRIDGE?

"Who's been sitting in my bed?"
   said the mama bear crossly.
"Who's been eating my chair?"
   said the baby bear weepily.
"Who's been sleeping in my porridge?"
   said the papa bear angrily.
"Wait a minute," said Goldilocks.

"Why can't you guys just stick
to the script? Now let's try it
again and this time, no messing around."

16

IN  MY PORRIDGE? *by Colin McNaughton*

ON YOUR HEAD BE IT!

If you're poor and in distress,
Without a bean and penniless,
Your head is cold, your nose is blue,
Then this is my headvice to you:
Wear a teapot, wear a shoe,
Lift it up, say "How-de-do!"
Wear a sock, wear a pan,
Wear a king-size baked bean can.
Wear a saucer, wear a cup,
Wear a flower pot, downside up.
Wear a bucket, wear a bowl,
Wear the tube from a toilet roll.
Wear a lampshade, add some stars,
Wear a fishbowl, man from Mars!

Wear a pie (not too hot!),
Wear a sooty chimneypot.
Wear a matchbox, wear a book,
For that literary look.
Wear an eggcup, plain or spotty,
Wear a washed-out baby's potty.
Wear a yellow traffic cone,
Wear a big, brass bass trombone.
Wear an orange rubber glove,
Wear a housetrained turtle-dove.
Wear a ball, a loaf of bread,
A ripe banana—use your head!
Your head's in the sand if you can't see it.
If you catch cold, ON YOUR HEAD BE IT!

THE CROCODILE'S BRUSHING HIS TEETH

The crocodile's brushing his teeth, I'm afraid,
This certainly means we're too late.
The crocodile's brushing his teeth, I'm afraid,
He has definitely put on some weight.
The crocodile's brushing his teeth, I'm afraid,
It really is, oh, such a bore.
The crocodile's brushing his teeth, I'm afraid,
He appears to have eaten grade four!

17

THE HAPPY HEDGEHOG

Deep in the heart of Dickon Woods lived a happy hedgehog named Harry.

Harry loved noise, so he made a big drum and he banged on the drum *tum-tum-te-tum*. A hedgehog called Helen was out in the woods. She heard *tum-tum-te-tum* and she liked it. So she made a drum and went off to join in the drumming. And so did a hedgehog named Norbert and another called Billy; they both made drums and followed the *tum-tum-te-tums*, until all of the hedgehogs with drums were gathered together at Harry's.

Tum-tum-te-tum went one drum; that was Harry.

Diddle-diddle-dum went

one drum; that was Helen.

Ratta-tat-tat went one drum; that was Norbert.

And *BOOM* went one drum; that was Billy.

Tum-tum-te-tum diddle-diddle-dum ratta-tat-tat   BOOM!

Tum-tum-te-tum diddle-diddle-

BAND

by **Martin Waddell**   illustrated by **Jill Barton**

and the dove, the frog and the toad and the spider and the dog who was lost in the woods. *Tum* went the band and they STOPPED!

"We want to play too!" said the others. "But we haven't got drums. So what can we do?" And nobody knew except Harry.

dum ratta-tat-tat   BOOM!
All the woods were humming and tumming with drumming. **"STOP!"** cried the pheasant, the owl and the bee, the mole from his hole and a badger called Sam and his mother, and the fox and the crow, the deer

Harry knew all about noise. So he said, "You can hum, you can hoot, you can buzz, you can whistle, you can clap, you can click, you can pop. We'll carry on with the drums."

And . . .

19

20

ba-zooo ba-zoooo

clack- clack

h-ka

ratta-tat-tat

diddle-diddle-

dum

BOOM

they did.

And the dog
who was lost
in the woods
just danced.

*Tum-tum-te-tum
diddle-diddle-dum
ratta-tat-tat*

BOOM!

21

A Little Boy Came

from
HARD-BOILED LEGS

by **Michael Rosen**   illustrated by **Quentin Blake**

A little boy came down to breakfast

with bananas stuck in his ears.

Everyone said hello to him

but he didn't even notice.

So his mom said, "Are you all right?"

but the little boy said nothing.

So his sister said,

"Are you all right?"

but the little boy

still said nothing.

Then his brother noticed that

he had bananas stuck in his ears, so he said,

22

Down to Breakfast

"Hey, you've got bananas stuck in your ears," and the little boy said, "What?"

So his brother said it again. "You've got bananas stuck in your ears," and the little boy said, "What?" So the brother shouted really loudly at him, "YOU'VE GOT BANANAS STUCK IN YOUR EARS!"

And the little boy shouted back,

"I'M SORRY, I CAN'T HEAR YOU. I'VE GOT BANANAS IN MY EARS!"

THE MOUSEHOLE CAT

— AN EXTRACT —

by
Antonia Barber

illustrated by
Nicola Bayley

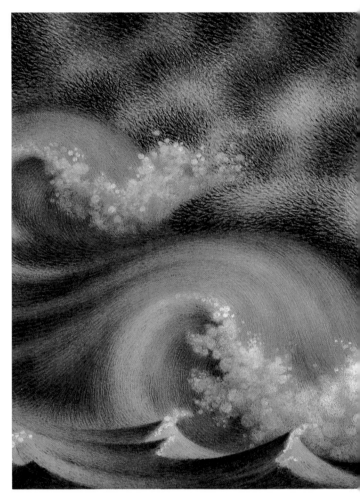

Swiftly the little boat passed through the Mousehole and out into the open sea.

Then the Great Storm-Cat played with them as a cat plays with a mouse. He would let them loose for a little as they fought their way toward the fishing grounds. Then down would come his giant cat's paw in a flurry of foam and water. But he did not yet strike to sink them, for that would have spoiled his sport.

When they reached the fishing grounds the sea was so rough that it was hard to put out the nets.

"I fancy you must sing again, Mowzer, my handsome," said Tom, "for your voice seems to soothe the sea like the sirens of old."

So Mowzer sang again, longer and louder than she had ever sung before. Indeed, old Tom was forced to block up his ears so that her siren song should not distract him from the business of fishing.

And again, the Great Storm-Cat

paused in his play and sang with her until the nets were safely shot.

All day they fished in a seething sea. The waves were so high and the clouds so low that they soon lost sight of the shore. And all the time the Great Storm-Cat played with the little boat, striking it and then loosing it, but never quite sinking it. And whenever his claws grew too sharp, Mowzer would sing to him to soften the edge of his anger. As evening came down they hauled in the nets. Into the belly of the boat tumbled ling and launces, scad, hake and fairmaids; enough fish for a whole cauldron of morgy-broth; enough pilchards for half a hundred star-gazy pies.

"Mowzer, my handsome, we are all saved," said old Tom, "if we can but bring this haul home to harbor."

Playschool Day
from
EMMA'S
Monster

by Marjorie Darke
illustrated by Shelagh McNicholas

Emma was going to playschool. She had been waiting to go for one, two, three weeks. Now here was the very first playschool day.

"What's it like at playschool?" Emma asked Dad as he helped put on her shoes.

"Fun," Dad said. "There's sand to dig in, and you can paint pictures, and go on the jungle gym, and sing songs, and there are lots of other children doing all these things with you. But we've talked about this before."

"I know." Emma wriggled her toes. "I just wanted to hear again."

Dad tied her laces.

"I don't think my monster is well enough to go to playschool today," Emma said.

"Your monster?" Dad asked as if he didn't know.

"He lives in that hole in the wall under my bed, remember?" Emma reminded him.

"Oh yes . . . of course." Dad got her jacket.

"He sneezed and sneezed last night. *Atchooooooo* . . . like that. He told me his throat was sore."

"In that case he'd better stay at home until he gets better." Dad held out the jacket. "Put your arms in."

Emma put one arm in. Then took it out. "I'd better stay too. In case he gets lonely. I'll go to playschool another day."

Dad thought for a moment. "If I were your monster, I'd want you to go to playschool. Then you could tell me all about it when you got home again."

Emma shook her head. "He wants to go *with* me. The very first day." She untied her laces and kicked off her shoes. "If I go by myself he'll be mad. He'll growl . . . *GRRRRR*. And bite with his big teeth . . . like that!" She snapped her teeth.

"He'll bite you, and me . . . he'll bite everybody."
"I see," said Dad. "We can't have that!" Picking up his newspaper, he sat down to read.

Emma watched him for a bit. Then she watched a fly crawl up the window and down again. Outside the sun had come out and somebody began to play a jingly tune. She knew that tune and who was playing it.

"Dad," she said. "Monster's sore throat might get better if he had ice cream. Then we could both go to play-school."

Dad looked at her over the top of his newspaper. "Is that so? But Monster isn't here. The ice cream would melt and drip on the floor with no-body to lick it."

"I'll get him while you get the ice cream," Emma said, and ran upstairs.

But when she looked under the bed there was nothing but dust.

She crept under the bed and peered down the hole in the wall. It was empty.

So she looked behind the door—only her bathrobe hanging on a hook.

She hunted in the bathroom and the linen closet. Nothing but soap in the bath and towels in the cupboard.

Emma went slowly back downstairs.
No Dad.

But two big, watery red eyes stared at her from a little crinkly face. Monster—sitting in Dad's chair! He smiled, showing his big green teeth, wrinkled his flat nose, and sneezed: "Atchoooooo!" like that—just as Dad came back holding an ice cream cone.

"Are you catching a cold?" Dad asked.

"Not me. That was Monster," Emma said. "And you should have brought two ice cream cones—one for me and one for him."

Dad looked around. "Is he here? I can't see him."

But Emma could. Monster had played a trick, shrunk very small and jumped to sit on the edge of the cone. He was licking ice cream with his long yellow tongue.

While they shared the ice cream, Emma told him all about playschool.

"You can dig in the sand and paint pictures and climb and sing and have fun with the children. Should we go together?"

Monster nodded his head so hard his wild, wild hair flew out like a mop.

Emma ate the last crumb of the cone. "We're ready to go to playschool now," she told Dad.

"Are you really sure?" he asked.

"Really, really, really!"

Emma began to put on her shoes.

Daley B.

Daley B. didn't know
what he was.
"Am I a monkey?"
he said.
"Am I a koala?
Am I a porcupine?"

Daley B. didn't know
where to live.
"Should I live in a cave?"
he said.
"Should I live in a nest?
Should I live in a web?"

Daley B. didn't know
what to eat.
"Should I eat fish?"
he said.
"Should I eat potatoes?
Should I eat worms?"

Daley B. didn't know
why his feet were so big.
"Are they for water-
skiing?" he said.

"Are they for the mice
to sit on?
Are they to keep the
rain off?"

Daley B. saw the birds
in the tree and decided
he would live in a tree.
Daley B. saw the
squirrels eating acorns
and decided he would
eat acorns.
But he still didn't know
why his feet were so big.

One day there was great
panic in the woods.
All the rabbits gathered
beneath Daley B.'s tree.
"You must come down
at once, Daley B.!" they
cried. "Jazzy D. is coming!"
"Who is Jazzy D.?" asked
Daley B.

by Jon Blake *illustrated by* Axel Scheffler

The rabbits were too excited to answer. They scattered across the grass and vanished into their burrows. Daley B. stayed in his tree, nibbled another acorn, and wondered about his big feet.

Jazzy D. crept out of the bushes. Her teeth were as sharp as broken glass, and her eyes were as quick as fleas. Jazzy D. sneaked around the burrows, but there was not a rabbit to be seen.

Jazzy D. looked up. Daley B. waved. Jazzy D. began to climb the tree. The other rabbits poked out their noses and trembled.

"Hello," said Daley B. to Jazzy D. "Are you a badger? Are you an elephant? Are you a duck-billed platypus?"

Jazzy D. crept closer.

"No, my friend," she whispered. "I am a weasel."

"Do you live in a pond?" asked Daley B.

"Do you live in a dam? Do you live in a kennel?"

Jazzy D. crept closer still.

"No, my friend," she hissed, "I live in the darkest corner of the woods."

"Do you eat cabbages?" asked Daley B.
"Do you eat insects? Do you eat fruit?"

Jazzy D. crept right up to Daley B.

"No, my friend," she rasped, "I eat rabbits! Rabbits like *you!*"

Daley B.'s face fell.
"Am I . . . a rabbit?" he stammered.

Jazzy D. nodded . . . and licked her lips . . .

and **leapt!**

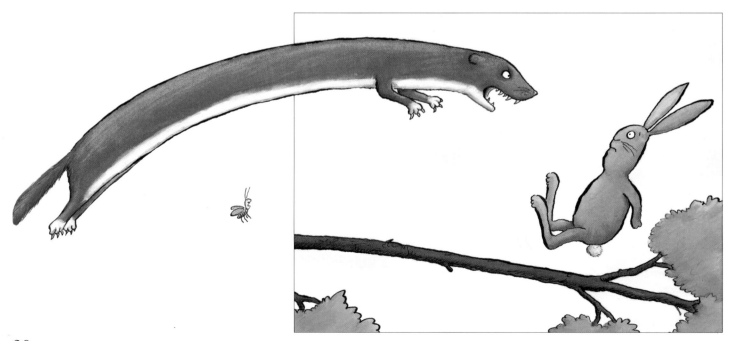

Daley B. didn't have to think. Quick as a flash, he turned his back, and kicked out with his massive feet. Jazzy D. sailed through the air, far far away, back where she came from.

The other rabbits jumped and cheered and hugged each other. "You're a hero, Daley B.!" they cried.

"That's funny," said Daley B. "I thought I was a rabbit."

THE STOPWATCH

Grandma said, "Here's a present, Tom."
It was a stopwatch. She started it. Tom
stopped it. It took him 9 seconds.
Tom ran out of Grandma's garden.
He ran home in 3 minutes 32 seconds.
He ate a snack in 2 minutes 6 seconds.
His sister Jan said it was too
disgusting to watch.
He got undressed and into the bath
and out again in 1 minute 43 seconds.
Jan said it was cheating not to use soap.
Next morning Tom held his breath for
32 seconds.
He stood on his head for 11 seconds.
Jan said, "Let's have a staring match."
Tom lost. He blinked after 41
seconds.
Then Tom lost his stopwatch.
He searched all over the house.
It took him a long time.
He didn't know how

by David Lloyd
illustrated by Penny Dale

long because he'd lost the stopwatch.
Jan came in. She said, "I can ride my bike to the store,
eat a Popsicle,
meet my
friend, go to
the park,
climb a tree, eat
another Popsicle,
and ride home
again in 32 minutes
58 seconds."
Tom and Jan fought
like cats and dogs.
Just then Grandma arrived.
She said, "Stop that
fighting! Stop it
at once!"
"Guess what, Grandma,"
Tom said. "We just
fought for exactly
7 minutes."

Sidney The Monster

by **David Wood**   illustrated by **Clive Scruton**

There was once a monster named Sidney.
"I'm bored," he said. "I feel like
some frightening."
So he rang a doorbell and hid.
When the lady opened the door . . .
Sidney jumped out and stuck
his tongue out at her. The lady screamed.

Sidney smiled. And went home.

"I'm still bored," said Sidney.
"I feel like some more frightening."
So he went to the supermarket and
pretended to be a frozen chicken.
When a customer tried to pick him up . . .
Sidney popped up and shouted, "BOO!"
The customer fainted.
Sidney giggled. And went home.
"I'm still bored," said Sidney.
"I'll go frightening again."
So he went to the park
and jumped into the pond with . . .
nothing on!
The park emptied.
Sidney laughed.
And went home.
"I'm still bored,"
said Sidney.
"And being
bored is boring.
Time for more frightening."
So he went to a school, looked through
a window and . . .

made a monstrously rude noise!

All the children ran out . . .

except for Millie.

Sidney stuck his tongue out at her.

Millie smiled.

Sidney shouted "BOO!" at her.

Millie giggled.

Sidney ran around with nothing on.

Millie laughed.

Sidney made a monstrously rude noise.

Millie roared.

"This isn't right," said Sidney.

"You're supposed to be frightened."

"I'm not frightened of you," said Millie.

"You're funny. Look!"

They smiled, they giggled,

they laughed,

they roared.

And

they

went

home.

"On your potty!"

BY VIRGINIA MILLER

One morning George padded
quietly over to Bartholomew's
bed to see if he was awake.
He asked softly,
"Are you awake, Ba?"
"Nah!" said Bartholomew.
George asked,
"Are you up, Ba?"
"Nah!" said Bartholomew.
George asked,
"Do you need your potty, Ba?"
"Nah!" said Bartholomew.
"Nah, nah, nah, nah, NAH!"
said Bartholomew.

"On your potty!"
George said in a big voice.
Bartholomew sat on his potty.
He tried . . . and he tried . . .
but nothing happened.
"Nah!" said Bartholomew
in a little voice.

"Never mind," said George.
"Out you go and play,
and be good."
"Nah!" said Bartholomew,
and off he went.
Suddenly Bartholomew
thought, On your potty!

He ran . . . and he ran . . .

and reached his potty . . .

as fast as he could . . .

just . . . in . . . time.

He padded proudly off
to find George,
who gave him a great big hug.

Strat and Chatto

by Jan Mark

illustrated by David Hughes

A rat ran up the fire escape and rapped at the cat flap. A cat looked out. His name was Chatto and it was his flap. "Good morning," said the rat, with his tail over his arm. "I hear you have a mouse problem. Can I be of assistance?"

"I certainly have a problem," said Chatto. "However, excuse my mentioning it, but aren't you of the mouse class yourself?"

"I am a rat," said the rat, "and you may call me Strat— short for Stratorat. I'm a high flyer."

He tried to look modest, but his whiskers twitched.

"Oh, a bat," said the cat.

"No, a rat," said Strat. "But some of my best friends are bats," he added. "We hang around together."

"Do you live in the belfry?" Chatto said.

"No," Strat said, "I have a pad in that place over there."

"The place where it says

C O N D E M N E D

on the door?" Chatto said. "That's a funny name for a house."

"It means 'Beautiful View' in Latin," Strat said. "Now, about these mice."

"One mouse," said Chatto. "I've eaten the others but this one eludes me. It sits on the fridge and drops lentils on my head."

"Let's have a look," said Strat, and he climbed through the cat flap.

Chatto lived in a good, clean kitchen with many corners and cracks in the floor.

"This is all right," said Strat. "I've always wanted a pad in a loft."

"Hello, Blotto," said a voice from high up.

"That's him," said Chatto. "That's my mouse. He pretends he doesn't know my name."

A lentil fell on his head. Strat sprang onto the trash can for a better view. The mouse lay at ease on top of the fridge with a pile of lentils beside him. He leaned on one elbow and yawned. "Poor old Blotto," he said. "Chatting with rats now, are we? How low can you sink?"

He dropped another lentil.

"That is surely a problem mouse," said Strat. "Give me a day to think about it."

"Can you get him out?" Chatto asked.

"Fat chance," said the mouse.

"Leave it to Strat," said the rat. "I have influence in high places." He ran back down the fire escape to his house, the one with

C O N D E M N E D

on the door.

That night Strat climbed to the belfry and yelled at the bats.

"Hush up," said the oldest bat.

"Ah, come on, now," said Strat.

"You'd do a favor for an old pal, wouldn't you?"

"What would we have to do?" asked the dangling bats.

"Only what you're doing now," said Strat, "but somewhere else, no sweat. A change will do you good. I'd like you to spend a few nights with a friend of mine, but don't tell him I sent you."

"Where do we find this friend?" said the oldest bat.

"He lives at the top of the fire escape," said Strat. "It's easy to get in. There's a bat flap."

Next day Strat ran up the fire escape.

Chatto came out.

"How's tricks?" said Strat.

"Worse and worse," said Chatto.

"Now I have bats hanging from the cup hooks."

"Give me a day to think about it," said Strat. "I have friends in low places," and he ran down the fire escape.

That night Strat went to the kitchen of the Corner Café where cockroaches feasted in the grease beneath the stove.

"Like a change of fat?" said Strat, to a lurking roach.

43

"What for?" said the cockroach.

"I hear tell there's a man coming with a can of Raid to spray you with," said Strat. "Better move on till he's gone."

"Where should we go?" asked the cockroach, quivering.

"Turn right at the fire escape," said Strat. "A friend of mine will put you up."

"Thanks for the tip," the cockroach said.

"Think nothing of it, pal," said Strat. "We vermin must stick together. Enjoy yourselves— there are plenty of lentils."

Next day Strat ran up the fire escape and out came Chatto.

"Fine help you've been," Chatto snapped. "Now I have cockroaches loafing in the corners and bats hanging from the cup hooks, not to mention lentils in my ears."

"Give me a day to think about it," said Strat, and he ran down the fire escape.

That night Strat slipped in at the back door of Jack's Bar and dug out the silverfish.

"How would you like a change of scenery?" said Strat.

"What for?" said the silverfish.

"I know a place that offers weekend breaks for people like you," said Strat. "There's a nice warm boiler and luxury cracks in the floor. Come along tomorrow and don't say I sent you."

Next day Strat ran up the fire escape and Chatto sprang out of the cat flap.

"When are you going to act?" cried Chatto. "I have bats on the cup hooks, cockroaches in the corners, and sixty-five silverfish slithering around in the cracks. I counted them all in. Also," he said, "that low-down mouse is still dropping lentils on my head from a great height."

"Give me a day to think about it," said Strat and he ran down the fire escape.

Next morning he met a toad on the road.

"Come with me," said Strat.

"I know someone who ought to meet you."

He ran up the fire escape with the toad at his heels. Out came Chatto like a bar of wet soap and screamed,

"DO SOMETHING!"

"Hang around," said Strat. "I'd like you to meet my loathsome friend."

Chatto took one look at the toad and moaned,

"I can't stand it." He fell flat on the fire escape and put his paws over his eyes.

Then Strat climbed in through the cat flap and yelled,

"EVERYBODY OUT!"

And out of the cat flap came the bats and the cockroaches and the silverfish.

They poured down the fire escape and away along the road, followed by the toad.

"There you are," said Strat, slapping his hands together.

"Go back in and see how it feels."

"Wonderful," said Chatto.

"Like old times again, just me and the mouse." A lentil fell on his head but he only blinked.

Next day Chatto and Strat sat on
the fire escape in the sun.
Along came a crane with a ball
and chain and knocked down
the house with
C O N D E M N E D
on the door.
"Didn't you live there once?"
said Chatto, when the dust
had settled.
"I believe I did," said Strat,
and he twirled his whiskers.
"What a good thing I moved."

"How can I reward you?"
"Put me on the payroll?"
Strat suggested. "Bed and board
and a bite of cheese on Sundays."
"Done!"
said Chatto,
and they
shook hands.

One day Pippo played in the mud and got really dirty. Mommy said we would have to put him in the machine with the wash.

I said good-bye to Pippo because I thought he might never come out of the machine. Poor Pippo went around and around. I hoped he didn't feel sick.

When Pippo came out of the machine, he was really wet. "Will Pippo ever get dry?" I asked Mommy. Mommy said he'd be dry soon if we hung him on the clothesline.

Washing Machine BY HELEN OXENBURY

I told Pippo he'd be dry by bedtime
if the sun came out and the
wind kept blowing.

The trouble is, I know Pippo's
going to get dirty again.
I can't keep him from
playing in muddy places.

"Quack!" said the

"Quack!" said the billy goat.

"Oink!" said the hen.

"Meow!" said the little chick

running in the pen.

"Gobble-gobble!" said the dog.

"Cluck!" said the sow.

"Whoo! Whoo!" the donkey said.

"Baa!" said the cow.

"Hee-haw!" the turkey cried.

The duck began to moo.

All at once the sheep went,

"Cock-a-doodle-doo!"

The owl coughed and cleared

his throat and he began to bleat.

"Bow-wow!" the rooster said

swimming in the heat.

"Cheep-cheep!" said the cat

as she began to fly.

48

billy goat

by Charles Causley

illustrated by Barbara Firth

"Farmer Brown has laid an egg—

that's the reason why."

OWL BABIES

Once there were three baby owls:

Sarah . . .   and Percy . . .

and Bill.

They lived in a hole
in the trunk of a tree
with their Owl Mother.

The hole had twigs and
leaves and owl feathers in it.
It was their house.

BY MARTIN WADDELL   ILLUSTRATED BY PATRICK BENSON

One night they woke up and
their Owl Mother was GONE.
"Where's Mommy?" asked Sarah.
"Oh my goodness!" said Percy.
"I want my mommy!" said Bill.

The baby owls *thought*
(all owls think a lot)—
"I think she's gone hunting,"
said Sarah.
"To get us our food!" said Percy.
"I want my mommy!" said Bill.

But their Owl Mother didn't come.
The baby owls came out of their
house and they sat on the tree
and waited.

A big branch for Sarah,
a small branch for Percy,
and an old piece of ivy for Bill.
"She'll be back," said Sarah.
"Back *soon!*" said Percy.
"I want my mommy!" said Bill.

It was dark in the woods and
they had to be brave, for things
moved all around them.

"She'll bring us mice and things
that are nice," said Sarah.
"I suppose so!" said Percy.
"I want my mommy!" said Bill.

They sat and they thought
(all owls think a lot)—
"I think we should *all* sit on *my*
branch," said Sarah.
And they did, all three together.

"Suppose she got lost," said Sarah.
"Or a fox got her!" said Percy.
"I want my mommy!"
said Bill.
And the baby owls
closed their owl eyes
and wished their
Owl Mother
would come.

51

AND SHE CAME.
Soft and silent, she swooped
through the trees to Sarah and
Percy and Bill.
"Mommy!" they cried, and they
flapped and they danced, and they
bounced up and down on their
branch.

"WHAT'S ALL THE FUSS?"
their Owl Mother asked.
"You knew I'd come back."
The baby owls thought
(all owls think a lot)—
"I knew it," said Sarah.
"And I knew it!" said Percy.
"I love my mommy!"
    said Bill.

Floss

by *Kim Lewis*

Floss was a young Border collie, who belonged to an old man in a town. She walked with the old man in the streets and loved playing ball with children in the park. "My son is a farmer," the old man told Floss. "He has a sheepdog who is too old to work. He needs a young dog to herd sheep on his farm. He could train a Border collie like you." So Floss and the old man traveled, away from the town with its streets and houses and children playing ball in the park. They came to the heather-covered hills of a valley, where nothing much grew except sheep. Somewhere in her memory, Floss knew about sheep. Old Nell soon showed her how to round them up. The farmer trained her to run wide and lie down, to walk on behind, to shed,

and to pen. She worked very hard to become a good sheepdog.

up balls in the park.
The farmer took Floss
up to the hill one day,
to see if she could gather
the sheep on her own.
She was rounding them
up when she heard a
sound. At the edge of
the field, the farmer's
children were playing,
with a brand-new black-
and-white ball.

Floss remembered all
about children. She ran
to play with their ball.
She showed off her best
nose kicks, her best
passes. She did her best
springs in the air.

But sometimes Floss
woke up at night, while
Nell lay sound asleep.

She remembered
about playing with
children and rounding

"Hey, Dad, look at this!"
yelled the children.
"Look at Floss!"

The sheep started drifting away. The sheep escaped through the gate and into the yard. There were sheep in the garden and sheep on the road.

"FLOSS! LIE DOWN!"

The farmer's voice was like thunder.

"You are supposed to work on this farm, not play!"

He took Floss back to the doghouse. Floss lay and worried about balls and sheep. She dreamed about the streets of a town, the hills of a valley, children and farmers, all mixed together, while Nell had to round up the straying sheep. But Nell was too old to work every day,

and Floss had to learn to take her place. She worked so hard to gather sheep well, she was too tired to dream anymore. The farmer was pleased and

ran Floss in the dog trials. "She's a good worker now," the old man said. The children still wanted to play with their ball. "Hey, Dad," they asked,

"can Old Nell play now?" But Nell didn't know about children and play.

"No one can play ball like Floss," they said. So the farmer gave it some thought. "Go on, then," whispered the farmer to Floss. The children kicked the ball high into the air. Floss remembered all about children. She ran to play with their ball. She showed off her best nose kicks, her best passes. She did her best springs in the air. And they all played ball together.

A Piece of Cake

by Jill Murphy

"I'm fat," said Mrs. Large.
"No you're not," said Lester.
"You're our cuddly mommy," said Laura.
"You're just right," said Luke.
"Mommy's got wobbly bits," said the baby.
"Exactly," said Mrs. Large. "As I was saying—I'm fat."

"We must all go on a diet," said Mrs. Large. "No more cake. No more cookies. No more potato chips. No more sitting around all day. From now on, it's healthy living."

"Can we watch TV?" asked Lester, as they trooped in from school.
"Certainly not!" said Mrs. Large. "We're all off for a nice healthy jog around the park." And they were.

"What's our snack, Mom?" asked Laura when they arrived home.

"Some nice healthy watercress soup," said Mrs. Large. "Followed by a nice healthy cup of water."
"Oh!" said Laura. "That sounds . . . nice."

"I'm just going to watch the news, dear," said Mr. Large when he came home from work.
"No you're not, dear," said Mrs. Large. "You're off for a nice healthy jog around the park, followed by your supper—a delicious fish with grated carrot."
"I can't wait," said Mr. Large.

It was awful. Every morning there was a healthy breakfast followed by exercises. Then there was a healthy snack followed by a healthy jog. By the time evening came everyone felt terrible.
"We aren't getting any thinner, dear," said Mr. Large.

"Perhaps elephants are meant to be fat," said Luke.
"Nonsense!" said Mrs. Large. "We mustn't give up now."
"Wibbly-wobbly, wibbly-wobbly," went the baby.

One morning a parcel arrived. It was a cake from Granny. Everyone stared at it hopefully. Mrs. Large put it into the cupboard on a high shelf. "Just in case we have visitors," she said sternly.

Everyone kept thinking about the cake. They thought about it during the healthy jog. They thought about it during supper. They thought about it in bed that night.
Mrs. Large sat up. "I can't stand it anymore," she said to herself. "I must have a piece of that cake."

58

Mrs. Large crept out of bed and went downstairs to the kitchen. She took a knife out of the drawer and opened the cupboard. There was only one piece of cake left!

"Ah ha!" said Mr. Large, seeing the knife. "Caught in the act!"

Mrs. Large switched on the light and saw Mr. Large and all the children hiding under the table.

"There *is* one piece left," said Laura in a helpful way.

Mrs. Large began to laugh. "We're all as bad as each other!" she said, eating the last piece of cake before anyone else did. "I do think elephants are meant to be fat," said Luke.

"I think you're probably right, dear," said Mrs. Large. "Wibbly-wobbly, wibbly-wobbly!" went the baby.

ALL PIGS ARE BEAUTIFUL

*by **Dick King-Smith** illustrated by **Anita Jeram***

I love pigs. I don't care if they're little pigs or big pigs, with long snouts or short snouts, with ears that stick up or ears that flop down. I don't mind if they're black or white or ginger or spotted. I just love pigs.

If you really twisted my arm and said, "You have to have a favorite kind of pig. What is it?" then I might have to say, "A black-and-white, spotted, medium-snouted, flop-eared pig that comes from Gloucestershire" . . . though of all the pigs I ever owned, my one particular favorite was a boar called Monty, who was a large white.

Monty never looked very white, because he lived out in the woods where there was a pond in which he liked to wallow—but he looked very large. And he was. I bought him as a youngster, but when he was full-grown he weighed six hundred pounds. Monty was so gentle. When I went out to feed him and his ten wives, he would come galloping through the trees at my call, a really monstrous and frightening sight to anyone who didn't know what a pushover he was.

Large White

Saddleback

British Lop

What he really loved, once he'd finished his slop, was to be scratched on the top of his head, between his big ears, and it always affected him in the same way. His eyes, with their long pale lashes, would close in ecstasy and slowly his hindquarters would sink down until he was sitting on his bottom like a huge dog. *Oh, this is lovely,* you could almost hear him thinking. *What more can life offer?* Most pigs aren't so fussy. Just having their backs scratched is enough for them—they squirm with pleasure. And of course you have to talk to them. Pigs, like people, enjoy a good chat, so don't just stand there saying nothing. "Piggy-piggy-piggy" will do if you don't happen to know the pig's name.

If I'm talking to a big fat sow and don't know what she's called, I usually call her "Mother" or "Mommy." They like that.

61

Tamworth

Large White

Large Black

Sows spend their lives having babies, lots of them, and they take as good care of them as your mom does of you. Well, almost. Trouble is, newborn piglets are so small that sometimes the sow lies down and squashes one. Your mother would never do that to you— I hope! Of course, while you're busy talking to pigs, telling them how wonderful they or their babies are, the pigs are talking back. Those who don't know much about them just hear grunts and squeaks, but there are all kinds of things a pig might be saying to you, if you understood the language, such as: "How kind of you to admire my children," or

"Scratch a little harder, please— up a little, a little to the left, down a little. Yes, that's it!" or "Well, no, actually you're not the first person to call me beautiful," or "This food

is really excellent, yum, yum. Thanks a lot."

But of course, pigs, like people, aren't always sunny and good-tempered, and you might hear: "Hurry up, you stupid two-legged creature, I'm starving and you're late!" or "Don't you dare pick

Gloucester Old Spot

Middle White

Berkshire

up one of my babies or I'll bite you!" (And do be careful— pigs have a horrible bite so don't take any chances.)

Pigs can be stubborn, like people, which makes them difficult to herd. A pig's insides are pretty much the same as ours, too. Heart and lungs and liver and kidneys and stomach— they're all in the same places as ours are, and pigs, like people, can eat meat or vegetables or both. Like people (or at any rate people who have been potty-trained), pigs have very clean habits and will never soil their own nests.

Have you noticed how often I've said that pigs are like people? That's one of the reasons I like them so much. There's one big difference, though. People can be good-looking or just ordinary-looking or plain ugly.

But all pigs are beautiful.

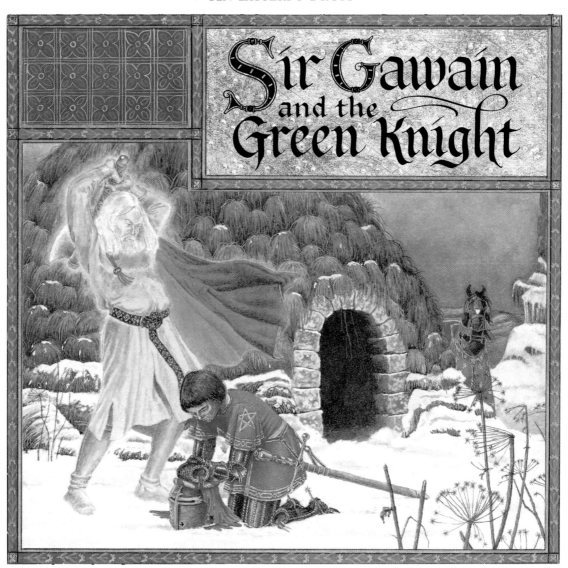

Sir Gawain and the Green Knight

WORDS BY SELINA HASTINGS ♦ ILLUSTRATED BY JUAN WIJNGAARD

THE TWO MEN rode in silence through the icy woods until the guide stopped suddenly. "Sir Gawain, we are almost at the Green Chapel, but I implore you not to go farther. This is a wild and dangerous place and the Green Knight is a terrible man. He has the strength of five and is a savage killer. Few men meet him and live to tell the tale. To continue on this path means certain death."

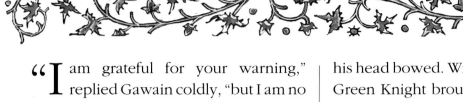

"I am grateful for your warning," replied Gawain coldly, "but I am no coward. There is no power on earth that will keep me from my encounter at the Green Chapel."

"So be it," said the guide. "Here is your helmet and your lance. If you follow the narrow track between those rocks, you will come to the Chapel."

Gawain spurred on Gringolet, riding right down into the ravine, but he saw no sign of any dwelling, only great jagged boulders rising up on either side. Then he caught sight of a little grass-covered mound. "Is this what I am looking for?" he thought, dismounting to examine it more closely. It seemed deserted, a small evil-looking hummock with an opening at either end. As Gawain walked around it, he heard a whirring, rushing noise coming at him from all sides.

"Who's there?" cried Gawain, startled.

"Stay where you are! And stand to receive the blow which I promised you." With these words the Green Knight appeared on the top of the hummock, whirling around his head a great axe, its shining blade honed to a deadly edge.

"Welcome, Sir Gawain," said the Knight, descending the hummock. "I see you are a man of your word. Remove your helmet. It is my turn to take aim at you."

Obediently Gawain took off his helmet and knelt before the Knight, his head bowed. With all his strength, the Green Knight brought the axe whistling down, but just in time Gawain shrank slightly to one side so that the blade missed him by a hair.

"What!" bellowed the Knight. "Are you afraid? I never flinched when I knelt before you. Surely you are not such a coward as to try to escape your due!"

"I shall not move the next time," Gawain said penitently. "If my head falls to the ground, I shall not flinch."

"Brace yourself then!" cried the Knight fiercely, brandishing his axe and making as if to bring it down. But at the last second he held back. "Now I shall put to the test the courage of King Arthur's famous knights. Now I shall see what kind of man you are."

"Stop threatening me and strike your blow!" said Gawain angrily. "You have my word I shall not flinch."

So up went the axe and down it flashed on the white skin of Gawain's neck. Although savage, it was a glancing blow which caught him only on the side of his neck.

When Gawain saw the blood spurt on the snow, he jumped to his feet, snatching up his sword and shield. Never in his life had he felt so light of heart. "Enough!" he cried. "Our bargain is complete! You cannot touch me now!"

Ragged Robin

Poems by *James Reeves*
illustrated by *Emma Chichester Clark*

I

Islands

I, with my mind's eye, see
Islands and indies fair and free,
Fair and far in the coral sea.

Out of the sea rise palmy shores;
Out of the shore rise plumy trees;
Out of each tree a feathered bird
Sings with a voice like which
  no voice was ever heard,
And palm and plume and feather
Blend and bloom together
In colors like the green
  of summer weather.

And in this island scene
There is no clash nor quarrel;
Here the seas wash
In shining fields of coral
Indies and isles that lie
Deep in my mind's eye.

An excerpt from

EAST O' THE SUN ·AND· WEST O' THE MOON

illustrated by

P.J. Lynch

O nce on a time there was a poor farmer who had so many children that he hadn't much of either food or clothing to give them. Pretty children they all were, but the prettiest was the youngest daughter, who was so lovely there was no end to her loveliness.

Well, one day, 'twas on a Thursday evening late at the fall of the year, the weather was so wild and rough outside that the walls of the cottage shook. It was cruelly dark, and rain fell and wind blew. There they all sat around the fire busy with this thing and that when, all at once, something gave three taps on the windowpane. Then the father went out to see what was the matter; and, when he got out-of-doors, what should he see but a big White Bear.

"Good evening to you," said the White Bear.

"The same to you," said the man.

"Will you give me your youngest daughter? If you will, I'll make you as rich as you are now poor," said the Bear.

Well, the man would not be at all sorry to be so rich; but still he thought he must have a bit of a talk with his daughter first, so he went in and told them how there was a great White Bear waiting outside who had given his word to make them so rich if he could only have the youngest daughter.

The lassie said "No!" outright. Nothing could get her to say anything else, so the man went out and settled it with the White Bear that he should come again the next Thursday evening and get an answer. In the meantime he talked to his daughter and kept on telling her of all the riches they would get, and how well off she would be herself; and so at last she thought better of it, and

and they came into a castle where there were many rooms all lit up; rooms gleaming with silver and gold. And there, too, was a table ready laid, and it was all as grand as grand could be. Then the White Bear gave her a silver bell; and when she wanted anything, she was only to ring it, and she would get it at once.

Well, after she had eaten and drunk, and evening wore on, she got sleepy after her journey, and thought she would like to go to bed, so she rang the bell; and she had scarce taken hold of it before she found herself in a chamber, where there was a bed made, as fair and white as anyone would wish to sleep in, with silken pillows, and curtains fringed with gold. All that was in the room was gold or silver. But when she had gone to bed and put out the light, a man came and laid himself alongside her. That was the White Bear, who threw off his beast shape at night; but she never saw him as a man, for he always came after she had put out the light, and before the day dawned he was up and off again.

washed and mended her rags, made herself as beautiful as she could, and was ready to start. I can't say her packing gave her much trouble. Next Thursday evening came the White Bear to fetch her, and she got upon his back with her bundle, and off they went. When they had gone part of the way, the White Bear said:

"Are you afraid?"

No! she wasn't.

"Well, mind and hold tight to my shaggy coat, and then there's nothing to fear," said the Bear. So she rode a long, long way, till they came to a great steep hill. There, on the face of it, the White Bear gave a knock, and a door opened,

HORATIO'S BED

All night Horatio could not sleep.

He tossed
and turned

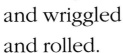

and wriggled
and rolled.

But he just could not
get comfortable.
"I'll go and ask James
what's the matter,"
he thought.
James was
busy drawing.
Horatio sat down.
"I couldn't sleep
all night," he said.
"Is it your bed?"
asked James.
"I haven't got
a bed," Horatio said.

"Then let's make you one,"
said James.
James took a clean sheet of paper
from his Useful Box and very
carefully drew a bed for Horatio.

by Camilla Ashforth

It was a big square bed with a leg at each corner. Then he took another sheet of paper and drew another bed for Horatio. This one was a big square bed with a leg at each corner too.

Horatio was very excited. He took one of James's drawings and tried to fold it into a bed. Then he climbed inside it and closed his eyes.

It wasn't very comfortable and when Horatio rolled over . . .

R R R I I I P P P !

James looked up. "That bed looks too hard to sleep on," he said and continued his drawing.

Horatio thought for a moment. Then he pulled some feathers out of James's pillow and made a big square bed with them.

But when he lay on it, the feathers tickled his nose.

AAACHOO! AAACHOO! AAACHOO!

He sneezed and sneezed.

71

James put down his pencil and
blew away the feathers.
James sat Horatio down on
his Useful Box.
"You wait here a minute," he said,
"while I just finish drawing your
bed." He had already drawn five
square beds and was getting very
good at them.
But when James turned away,
Horatio slipped down from the
Useful Box. He wanted to see what
James kept inside.
He made some steps up to the lid.
He pushed it open and leaned in.
There were all sorts of things —
buttons, brushes, keys, and
clothespins, clock wheels,
clips, and little pieces of string.
Horatio looked for a bed.
He couldn't find anything that
looked like James's drawings.

But he did find a big red sock.
"Look, James!" he cried.
"I've found your other sock!"
James did not seem very pleased.
He didn't like anyone looking in
his Useful Box. Not even Horatio.
Very quietly and carefully he started
to put away his Useful Things.
When he had finished, he closed
the lid and looked for Horatio.
"Now we can make you
a bed," he said.

But there was no need, because
Horatio was fast asleep.
His bed was not
square and it did
not have a leg
at each corner.

But for little Horatio,
it was just right.

73

The Owl and the Pussy Cat

by Edward Lear   illustrated by Louise Voce

The Owl and
    the Pussy Cat
    went to sea
In a beautiful
    pea-green boat,
They took some honey,
    and plenty of money,
Wrapped up in a
    five pound note.
The Owl looked up
    to the stars above,
And sang
    to a small guitar,
"O lovely Pussy!
    O Pussy, my love,
What a beautiful
    Pussy you are,
You are, you are!
What a beautiful
    Pussy you are!"

Pussy said to the Owl,
    "You elegant fowl!
How charmingly
    sweet you sing!
O let us be married!
    too long we have
    tarried:
But what shall we
    do for a ring?"

They sailed away,

for a year and a day,

To the land where

the Bong Tree grows,

74

And there in a wood
  a Piggy-wig stood
With a ring
  at the end of his nose,
His nose, his nose,
With a ring at the end
  of his nose.

"Dear Pig,
  are you willing
  to sell for one shilling
Your ring?"
  Said the Piggy, "I will."
So they took it away,
  and were married
  next day
By the Turkey
  who lives on the hill.

They dined on mince,
  and slices of quince,
Which they ate
  with a runcible spoon;
And hand in hand, on
  the edge of the sand,
They danced by the light
  of the moon,
The moon, the moon,
They danced by the light
  of the moon.

WE'RE THE NOISY DINOSAURS!

BY JOHN WATSON

WE'RE THE NOISY DINOSAURS, CRASH, BANG, WALLOP!
WE'RE THE NOISY DINOSAURS, CRASH, BANG, WALLOP!
IF YOU'RE SLEEPING, WE'LL WAKE YOU UP!
WE'RE THE NOISY DINOSAURS, CRASH, BANG, WALLOP!

WE'RE THE HUNGRY DINOSAURS, UM, UM, UM!
WE'RE THE HUNGRY DINOSAURS, UM, UM, UM!
WE WANT EGGS WITH JAM ON TOP!
WE'RE THE HUNGRY DINOSAURS, UM, UM, UM!

WE'RE THE BUSY DINOSAURS, PLAY, PLAY, PLAY!
WE'RE THE BUSY DINOSAURS, PLAY, PLAY, PLAY!
WE'VE GOT TOYS TO SHARE WITH YOU!
WE'RE THE BUSY DINOSAURS, PLAY, PLAY, PLAY!

WE'RE THE HAPPY DINOSAURS, HA, HA, HA!
WE'RE THE HAPPY DINOSAURS, HA, HA, HA!
WE TELL JOKES AND TICKLE EACH OTHER!
WE'RE THE HAPPY DINOSAURS, HA, HA, HA!

WE'RE THE DANCING DINOSAURS, QUICK, QUICK, SLOW!
WE'RE THE DANCING DINOSAURS, QUICK, QUICK, SLOW!
HOLD OUR HANDS BUT DON'T STEP ON OUR FEET!
WE'RE THE DANCING DINOSAURS, QUICK, QUICK, SLOW!

WE'RE THE THIRSTY DINOSAURS, SLURP, SLURP, GLUG!
WE'RE THE THIRSTY DINOSAURS, SLURP, SLURP, GLUG!
WE'LL DRINK THE SEA AND YOUR BATHWATER TOO!
WE'RE THE THIRSTY DINOSAURS, SLURP, SLURP, GLUG!

WE'RE THE ANGRY DINOSAURS, ROAR, ROAR, ROAR!
WE'RE THE ANGRY DINOSAURS, ROAR, ROAR, ROAR!
GET OUT OF OUR WAY OR WE'LL EAT YOU UP!
WE'RE THE ANGRY DINOSAURS, ROAR, ROAR, ROAR!

WE'RE THE NAUGHTY DINOSAURS, BAD, BAD, BAD!
WE'RE THE NAUGHTY DINOSAURS, BAD, BAD, BAD!
WE SAY SORRY AND PROMISE TO BE GOOD!
WE'RE THE NAUGHTY DINOSAURS, BAD, BAD, BAD!

WE'RE THE QUIET DINOSAURS, SHH, SHH, SHH!
WE'RE THE QUIET DINOSAURS, SHH, SHH, SHH!
WE READ BOOKS AND PLAY HIDE-AND-SEEK!
WE'RE THE QUIET DINOSAURS, SHH, SHH, SHH!

WE'RE THE DIRTY DINOSAURS, SCRUB, SCRUB, SCRUB!
WE'RE THE DIRTY DINOSAURS, SCRUB, SCRUB, SCRUB!
WE WASH OUR NECKS AND BRUSH OUR TEETH!
WE'RE THE DIRTY DINOSAURS, SCRUB, SCRUB, SCRUB!

WE'RE THE SLEEPY DINOSAURS, YAWN, YAWN, YAWN!
WE'RE THE SLEEPY DINOSAURS, YAWN, YAWN, YAWN!
SEND US TO BED WITH A GREAT BIG KISS!
WE'RE THE SLEEPY DINOSAURS, YAWN, YAWN, YAWN!

WE'RE THE DREAMING DINOSAURS, SNORE, SNORE, SNORE!
WE'RE THE DREAMING DINOSAURS, SNORE, SNORE, SNORE!
WE DREAM OF MONSTERS AND CHILDREN TOO!
WE'RE THE DREAMING DINOSAURS, SNORE, SNORE, SNORE!

79

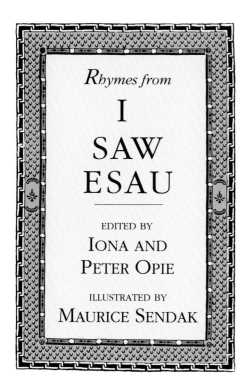

Rhymes from

I SAW ESAU

EDITED BY
IONA AND
PETER OPIE

ILLUSTRATED BY
MAURICE SENDAK

Moses supposes
his toeses are roses,
But Moses supposes
erroneously.
For Moses he knowses
his toeses aren't roses,
As Moses supposes
his toeses to be.

Moods and Tenses
Bother my senses;
Adverbs, Pronouns,
Make me roar.
Irregular Verbs
My sleep disturb,
They are a regular bore.

Different people have
different 'pinions;

Some like apples
and some like inions.

This book is one thing,
My fist is another;
Steal not the one
For fear of the other.

The rain
it raineth
all around
Upon the just and unjust fella;
But chiefly on the just because
The unjust
stole
the just's
umbrella.

There was a man
who always wore
A saucepan on his head.
I asked him what
he did it for—
"I don't know why," he said.
"It always makes
my ears so sore,
I am a foolish man.
I think I'll have
to take it off,
And wear a frying pan."

Rain,
rain,
go
away,

Come
another
summer's
day;

Tom tied a kettle
   to the tail of a cat;
Jill put a stone
   in the blind man's hat;
Bob threw his grandmother
   down the stairs—

And they all grew up ugly
   and nobody cares.

I saw Esau kissing Kate,
The fact is we all three saw;
   For I saw him,
   And he saw me,
   And she saw
      I
     SAW
    ESAU.

Rain,
   rain,
      pour
         down,

And come
   no more
      to our
         town.

Let's Go Home, Little Bear

by Martin Waddell ✳ *illustrated by* Barbara Firth

Once there were two bears. Big Bear and Little Bear. Big Bear is the big bear and Little Bear is the little bear.

They went for a walk in the woods. They walked and they walked and they walked until Big Bear said, "Let's go home, Little Bear."

So they started back home on the path through the woods.

PLOD PLOD PLOD went Big Bear, plodding along.

Little Bear ran on in front, jumping and sliding and having great fun.

And then . . . Little Bear stopped and he listened and then he turned around and he looked.

"Come on, Little Bear," said Big Bear, but Little Bear didn't stir.

"I thought I heard something!" Little Bear said.

"What did you hear?" said Big Bear.

"Plod, plod, plod," said Little Bear.

"I think it's a Plodder!"

Big Bear turned around and he listened and looked.

No Plodder was there.

"Let's go home, Little Bear," said Big Bear. "The plod was my feet in the snow."

They set off again on the path through the woods.

PLOD PLOD PLOD went Big Bear with Little Bear walking beside him, just glancing a bit, now and again.

And then . . . Little Bear stopped and he listened and then he turned around and he looked.

"Come on, Little Bear," said Big Bear, but Little Bear didn't stir.

"I thought I heard something!" Little Bear said.

"What did you hear?" said Big Bear.

"Drip, drip, drip," said Little Bear. "I think it's a Dripper!"

Big Bear turned around, and he listened and looked.

No Dripper was there.

"Let's go home, Little Bear," said Big Bear.

"That was the ice as it dripped in the stream."

They set off again on the path through the woods.

PLOD PLOD PLOD went Big Bear with Little Bear closer beside him.

And then . . . Little Bear stopped and he listened and then he turned around and he looked. "Come on, Little Bear," said Big Bear, but Little Bear didn't stir.

"I know I heard something this time!" Little Bear said.

"What did you hear?" said Big Bear.

"Plop, plop, plop," said Little Bear. "I think it's a Plopper."

Big Bear turned around, and he listened and looked.

No Plopper was there.

"Let's go home, Little Bear," said Big Bear.

"That was the snow plopping down from a branch."

PLOD PLOD PLOD went Big Bear along the path through the woods. But Little Bear walked slower and slower and at last he sat down in the snow.

"Come on, Little Bear," said Big Bear. "It is time we were both back home."

But Little Bear sat and said nothing.

"Come on and be carried," said Big Bear.

Big Bear put Little Bear high up on his back, and set off down the path through the woods.

WOO WOO WOO "It's only the wind, Little Bear," said Big Bear and he walked on down the path.

CREAK CREAK CREAK "It's only the trees, Little Bear," said Big Bear and he walked on down the path.

PLOD PLOD PLOD "It is only the sound of my feet again," said Big Bear, and he plodded on and on and on until they came back home to their cave.

Big Bear and Little Bear went down into the dark, the dark of their own Bear Cave.

"Just stay there, Little Bear," said Big Bear, putting Little Bear in the Bear Chair with a blanket to keep him warm. Big Bear stirred up the fire from the embers and lighted the lamps and made the Bear Cave all cozy again.

"Now tell me a story," Little Bear said.

And Big Bear sat down in the Bear Chair with Little Bear curled on his lap. And he told a story of Plodders and Drippers and Ploppers and the sounds of the snow in the woods, and this Little Bear and this Big Bear plodding all the way . . .

HOME.

85

FIRST Things FIRST

ONE, Two, three, four, five,
Once I caught a fish alive,
Six, seven, eight, nine, ten,
Then I let it go again.

86

by CHARLOTTE VOAKE

Why did you let it go?
Because it bit my finger so.
Which finger did it bite?
This little finger on the right.

BIRDS BEASTS A·N·D FISHES

Poems selected by Anne Carter
illustrated by Reg Cartwright

THE TIGER

Tiger! Tiger! burning bright
In the forests of the night,
What immortal hand or eye
Could frame thy fearful symmetry?

In what distant deeps or skies
Burnt the fire of thine eyes?
On what wings dare he aspire?
What the hand dare seize the fire?

And what shoulder, and what art,
Could twist the sinews of thy heart?
And when thy heart began to beat,
What dread hand? and what dread feet?

What the hammer? what the chain?
In what furnace was thy brain?
What the anvil? what dread grasp
Dare its deadly terrors clasp?

When the stars threw down their spears,
And water'd heaven with their tears,
Did he smile his work to see?
Did he who made the Lamb make thee?

Tiger! Tiger! burning bright
In the forests of the night,
What immortal hand or eye,
Dare frame thy fearful symmetry?

William Blake

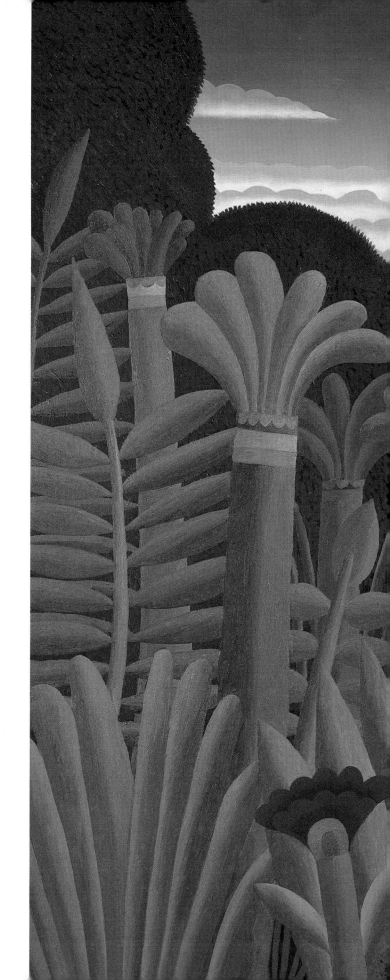

I Bought My Love a

I bought my love a tabby cat,
A tabby cat, a tabby cat,
My love made him a velvet hat
To wear when we were wed.

I bought my love a billy goat,
A billy goat, a billy goat,
My love made him a woolen coat
To wear when we were wed.

I bought my love a big, fat pig,
A big, fat pig, a big, fat pig,
My love made him a fancy wig
To wear when we were wed.

I bought my love an old gray goose,
An old gray goose, an old gray goose,
My love made him some dainty shoes
To wear when we were wed.

I bought my love a little mule,
A little mule, a little mule,
My love made him a silken shawl
To wear when we were wed.

I bought my love a talking crow,
A talking crow, a talking crow,
My love made him a handsome bow
To wear when we were wed.

Tabby Cat

*by **Colin West***
*illustrated by **Caroline Anstey***

And on the day that we were wed,
That we were wed, that we were wed,
I turned to my true love and said,
"Oh, what a sight to see . . .

"A tabby cat who wears a hat,
A billy goat who wears a coat,
A big, fat pig who wears a wig,
An old gray goose who wears new shoes,
A little mule who wears a shawl,
A talking crow who wears a bow,

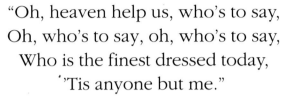

"Oh, heaven help us, who's to say,
Oh, who's to say, oh, who's to say,
Who is the finest dressed today,
'Tis anyone but me."

But since that day when we were wed,
When we were wed, when we were wed,

My love makes clothes for me instead,
As pretty as can be!

91

In The Middle Of The Night

by Kathy Henderson
illustrated by Jennifer Eachus

A long time after bedtime
when it's very very late
when even dogs dream
and there's deep sleep
breathing through the house

when the doors are locked
and the curtains drawn
and the shops are dark
and the last train's gone
and there's no more traffic
    in the street
because everyone's asleep

then

the window cleaner comes
to the main street shop fronts
and polishes the glass
in the street-lit dark

and a big truck rumbles past
on its way to the dump
loaded with the last
of the old day's trash.

On the twentieth floor
of the office tower
there's a lighted window
and high up there
another night cleaner's
vacuuming the floor
working nights on her own
while her children sleep at home.

And down in the dome
of the observatory
the astronomer who's
waited all day
for the dark

is watching the good black sky
at last
for stars and moons
and spikes of light
through her telescope
in the middle of the night
while everybody sleeps.

At the bakery
the bakers in their floury clothes
mix dough in machines
for tomorrow's loaves of bread

and out by the gate
rows of parked vans wait
for their drivers to come
and take the newly baked
bread to the shops
for the time when the
bread eaters wake.

Across the town at the hospital
where the nurses watch in the
dim-lit wards
someone very old shuts their eyes
and dies
breathes their very last breath
on their very last night.

Yet not far away on another floor
after months of waiting
a new baby's born
and the mother and the father
hold the baby and smile
and the baby looks up
and the world's just begun
but still everybody sleeps.

Now through the silent station
past the empty shops

and the office towers
past the sleeping streets
and the hospital
a train with no windows
goes rattling by

and inside the train the sorters sift
urgent letters and packets on the
late-night shift
so tomorrow's mail will arrive
in time
at the towns and the villages
down the line.

And the mother
with the wakeful child in her arms
walking up and down
and up and down
and up and down
the room
hears the train as it passes by
and the cats in the yard
and the night owl's flight
and hums hushabye and hushabye
we should be asleep now
you and I
it's late and time to close your eyes

it's the middle of the night.